50 FACTS ABOUT MONEY

"Mastering the Art of Wealth, Finance, and Prosperity"

By

SAMUEL ODAME-ANSA

Copyright © 2024

50 FACTS ABOUT MONEY

Unless otherwise identified, Scripture quotations are taken from
HOLY BIBLE, NEW INTERNATIONAL VERSION (NIV)

Copyright © 2024 SAMUEL ODAME-ANSA

ISBN: 979-834-0-62974-6

All rights reserved. No part of this publication may be reproduced, stored in a retrieval system, or transmitted in any form or by any means, electronic, mechanical, photocopying, recording, or otherwise, except for brief quotations in critical reviews or articles, without prior written permission from the author.

Please direct your inquiries to:

RABBI ODAME-ANSA

(+233) 24 256 0562

Published by

ODAME-ANSA & ASSOCIATES

P. O. Box NK 225, North Kaneshie, Accra, Ghana.

(+233) 0275858710, (+233) 0202525262

Email: odameansa@gmail.com

CONTENTS

Acknowledgement……………………………………........ v

Dedication……………………………………………............vi

Introduction…………………………………………….......vii

Chapter 1: Understanding Money……………….............1

- Definition of Money
- Facts #1-5: Laws, Problem-Solving, Skill, Value, Inspiration

Chapter 2: Money Flows………………………….............13

- Facts #6-10: Solutions, Energy, Productivity, Availability, Abundance

Chapter 3: Making Money……………………….............23

- Facts #11-15: Ordered Environment, Creating Money, Giving Birth, Growth, Equality

Chapter 4: Money Management…………………….........29

- Facts #16-20: Means to an End, Creating Assets, Liabilities, Circulation, Spending

Chapter 5: Financial Mindset………………….........39

- Facts #21-25: Financial Richness, Risk, Medium of Exchange, Keeping Money, Losing Money

Chapter 6: Breaking Financial Barriers..................48

- Facts #26-30: Income, Expenditure, Cause and Effect, Choice, Existing Money

Chapter 7: Smart Financial Decisions...................56

- Facts #31-35: Selling Something, Saving, Long-Term Gains, Financial Intelligence, Expense Reduction

Chapter 8: Investment Strategies........................62

- Facts #36-43: Limiting Losses, Delayed Gratification, Inflation Hedge, Risky Commodities, Liquid Assets, Passive Investment

Chapter 9: Wealth Building................................71

- Facts #44-48: Loan Repayment, Investment Completion, Respect for Money, Difficulty of Making Money

Chapter 10: Financial Discipline.........................80

- Facts #49-50: Buying What You Need, Taking Action

ACKNOWLEDGEMENT

I wish to express my heartfelt gratitude to the following individuals for their unwavering support throughout my Ministry assignment:

- Madam Joycelyn Adwoa Serwah Adomako (aka Auntie Serwah)
- Madam Beltra Baiden Afua Krah
- Pastor Enoch Annor Baffour
- The dedicated members of Grace House Chapel International

I pray that the Lord will richly bless each of you for your contributions to my journey.

DEDICATION

To GOD ALMIGHTY

INTRODUCTION

Money is a commodity that is very important in the life of every human being. It is so important that many people have allowed themselves to be enslaved by it; others have gone to jail because of it. Many people are ready to kill for it, others fight because of it, and many have had sleepless nights because of money. A lot of marriages have collapsed and others are on the verge of collapsing just because of money.

People are ready to do any kind of job for it, some have become slaves and it has turned some people into beggars. Some Pastors have been enslaved by it and I can boldly say that, when it comes to the issue of money, only few people can be found very innocent.

Issues and problems that are related to money I believe are a lot on this earth than any other related issues and problems. People spend sleepless nights thinking of how to break their economic barriers.

Destinies have been sold for money, and the most tragic aspect is that money often silences the truth.

When money speaks, the truth is concealed until many years have passed. In our world, those who have money rule, while those who do not have money are ruled. As the Bible says, *"money answers all things"* (Ecclesiastes 10:19), and just as wisdom is powerful, so is money. Money truly empowers, showcasing its immense power in our world.

No one can get fulfilled without it; it is the driving force of every great achievement in all aspect of human life and the lack of it can limit you in so many ways. It is the answer to so many questions.

The greatest book on the surface of this earth; the Bible says money answers all things. This means that, the lack of money leaves a lot of questions unanswered in one's life.

I would like to say that, each one of us should do his or her best to have enough of it.

Well, even though I have said all these things about money, money is not an end in itself; rather, it is a means to an end. That is why we can hear of some rich people committing suicide. The mere fact of having money does not bring you to an end or to an expected end.

Rather money can help you get to where you would like to be in the future. Money only empowers you to become the kind of person you are. If you like drinking, money will empower you to drink more, if you like giving; money will empower you to give more. If you like learning, money will empower you to learn more, if you like buying; money will empower you to buy more. Money only empowers you to do what you are already.

Chapter One:

UNDERSTANDING MONEY

- Definition of Money
- Facts #1-5: Laws, Problem-Solving, Skill, Value, Inspiration

WHAT IS MONEY?

Understanding what money is, is crucial before attempting to make it. Knowing the definition of money makes the process of earning it much easier. As the saying goes, "you can't do what you don't know." The more you want to achieve, the more you need to know. Therefore, defining money in a way that simplifies the process of making it is essential.

Money is the reward for solving a problem. In other words, it is the returns for solving a problem. It is what you receive or gain for providing someone with a solution. So, if you provide a solution to only two people, then it is only two people who will reward you with money.

The bigger the problem you solve, the bigger the money you will make, and the smaller the problem you solve, the smaller the money you will make. A lot of problems exist, and people are looking for solutions to them. The good news is that whenever you are able to solve their problems, they reward you with money. The more problems you solve for people, the more they reward you with money, and vice versa.

For example, consider the woman who sells food by the roadside. She is solving the problem of hunger. When you feel hungry, you have a problem that needs to be solved. The woman, who got up early to cook and prepare the food, is there to solve your hunger problem. Because you are hungry, you go to her for food, and after serving you, you reward her with an amount of money. This is how money is made.

Similarly, the secretary in the office is solving a problem for the boss by providing administrative support. In return, she is rewarded with an amount of money at the end of the month. This illustrates how money is earned by solving problems and providing value to others.

The banker would define money as a medium of exchange, which I totally agree with. However, I have a crucial question: HOW DO I MAKE THE MONEY BEFORE I USE IT TO EXCHANGE FOR SOMETHING? This is what they failed to teach us. We were only taught how to spend money, not how to make it. That is why I created this booklet, '50 FACTS ABOUT MONEY'.

Building on this question, let us explore the fundamental principle of making money. In principle, we make money by solving problems. So, the question is, how many problems are you solving? The amount of money you can make is directly proportional to the number of problems you can solve. I firmly believe that every individual on this earth should be taught basic knowledge about money: how to make it, keep it, invest it, grow it, spend it, and enjoy it. I call this 'The Six Arms of Money'.

FACT #1:

Money Is Governed by Laws

The fact is that money is governed by universal laws. Whether at home, at work, in your community, city, nation, or across international borders, MONEY FUNCTIONS AND IS GOVERNED BY SYSTEMS. Regardless of race, faith, or creed, specific principles control money, just as they do various aspects of life. No one can escape this reality.

To make money, one must obey these governing laws. Ample money is available for those who know how to acquire and retain it. Making money is easy; however, understanding how to make it is the challenge. That is where the laws of money come in, which is why I created this booklet.

I encourage you to study and memorize these principles thoroughly. Remember, knowledge is power to succeed.

FACT #2:

Money Is The Reward For Solving A Problem

As I mentioned in the definition of money, all monies made by individuals or groups have been earned through this principle. They identified a problem, found the best solution, and people paid for it. This method remains fundamental way of making money. If you want to make money, master the solution to a particular problem or problems and find ways to solve them. The more problems you solve, the more money you can make.

You do not always need to think of a new solution; you can import or transfer someone else's solution from one place to another. You can also study and improve on existing solutions to make them cheaper and better, then give them a new name. You do not necessarily need to invent something new.

For instance, most soft drinks have the same ingredients, with differences in colouring and naming. Beverages also have similar ingredients with some additions or subtractions and brand names to appeal to consumers. This illustrates that there is nothing new under the sun; it is just additions and subtractions of existing things.

With this explanation, you have no excuse to remain poor or in need. There are many problems in Ghana, Africa, and the world, and your duty is to find solutions. You have two options: come up with your own solution or learn from others, duplicate their success, and make your share of money.

One major character of money is that money flows but to certain strategic areas. I can boldly say that all things being equal, anyone or group of individuals who will position themselves in any of these areas will have money flowing to them.

FACT #3:

Money Flows To Where There Is Skill

Money flows to where Skill is displayed. Skill is a special ability that enables someone to do something very well. This special ability is gained by learning and practicing something over a period of time. So, anyone who wants to make a sustainable income must try to display a sustainable skill in whatever they are doing. Skill will make one very effective in bringing about good and desired results in whatever they do.

As said earlier, skill is acquired by submitting yourself to learn from other skilful individuals or a group of individuals. The next important thing anyone with skill should do is to make all the effort to let as many people as they can know what they are capable of doing.

In some cases, they have to sacrifice and do it for free to prove a point. Skill has a magnetic force that attracts people, and as they come and get the results they are looking for, they become satisfied and get rewarded with money.

They also start introducing others to you who will also reward you with money after getting the results they seek for. That is how money is made. Money flows to where there is skill, no matter where the person may be hiding.

Let us take, for example, six food vendors preparing the same food on the same street. I trust that the one who prepares the food with skill will make more sales than the rest. More people will buy her stuff, and this means that more money will flow to her.

This principle applies in all other fields of money making. People are ready to pay for skill, in other words, good and desired results. This is a fact about making money.

If you need more money, add to your life and career more skill. Do the right things and do them well, satisfy your customers, give them the desired results they need, and they will come again and again, meaning money will also come again and again.

FACT #4:

Money Flows To Where Value Is Created

Money flows to where there is VALUE. The reason is that I am yet to see or meet a person who does not appreciate something that will be Useful, Helpful, and Important to them. That is exactly what value means.

Value in simple terms is how useful, how helpful, and how important something or someone is to you in comparison to other things or persons. Value is the worth of something as compared to something of the same kind. We are saying money also flows to such an Area.

Everyone is ready to pay for Value. If the thing will be useful to him, he will pay for it, if it will be helpful to him, he is bound to pay for it and lastly if it is important to him, he has no choice, he will pay for it.

It will surprise you to know that what influences some people to buy is not the price of the item but the value on it. Many become colour and racial blind when it comes to value. That is why you find Africans working in some key positions in some parts of the world. People value people who can create value.

If indeed you want money, then one thing you must learn doing, is to create VALUE for people and the only way you can create value for people, is to make the effort to add value to your life. Educate yourself, learn and become highly informed, research, ask questions, follow experienced people, read their books etc. That is how you can add value to your life.

There is a saying that "If You Take Out of Your Pocket into Your Head, Your Head Will Pay Your Pocket Back." No one can create sustainable wealth without first creating sustainable value. If you can create things that will be important to someone, helpful to someone and useful to someone, then expect money to flow to you. There is no two ways about that.

FACT #5:

Money Flows to Where There is Inspiration and Ideas

Money flows to where there is INSPIRATION AND IDEAS. An idea is that which is seen in the mind's eye. A plan, an object, an image, a style, a design, a model, a concept etc. The dresses we put on are people's ideas and inspirations, the cars we drive, the buildings, the mobile phones, the sachet water business, the shoes we wear, the books people write for us to read, the music we enjoy etc are all people's inspiration and ideas.

Inspirations and ideas come about by thinking. That is using the mind to see things that do not yet exist and then bringing what you see in the mind into existence. Well, what I am saying is this, money flows to where there is inspiration and ideas. The good news is that, you can also come out with an idea or an inspiration and money will start flowing to you.

Chapter Two:

MONEY FLOWS

- Facts #6-10: Solutions, Energy, Productivity, Availability, Abundance

FACT #6:

Money Flows to Where There is Solutions

Money flows to where SOLUTION IS PROVIDED. Solution is the answer one gives to a problem. Man is surrounded with a lot of problems and difficulties that needs solutions and, in most cases, when people find themselves in such situations, they are ready to pay any amount so that they can come out of their problems. For instance, if a close relative is seriously ill to the point of death, you will be ready to pay any amount you would be charged to a Doctor who has the solution to that illness and can provide it. That is one of the ways one can make money, by providing solutions.

This is what it means to provide a solution

- To explain or clear up the difficulties one is facing
- To be able to bring about the required result one is looking for

- To be able to work out things better for someone
- To be able to remove the perplexity one is going through
- To be able to bring about a relief

Whenever, one is able to do any of the above, it will mean that the person is providing solution and there is no two ways about that, money will flow to such a person.

FACT #7:

Money Flows To Where There Is Energy

Money flows to where there is ENERGY. Energy is the inner power that one possesses to do a lot of work. It is also the power which one can use to work and thirdly, it is the power which can do work. Every work that needs to be done needs a certain degree of energy before the work can be done.

Anyone who has the energy and is ready to provide it, either by man power energy, mechanical energy, electrical energy, solar energy, mental energy, or by any other means applicable, can have money flowing to them. However, relying on man power energy can limit one's earning potential, especially with age. Money flows to where energy is provided, and exploring various forms of energy can unlock greater financial opportunities.

FACT #8 :

Money Flows To Where There Is Productivity

Money flows to where there is productivity; the ability to bring about the desired results. There is always an actual result required of you, and anytime you are able to bring about the required results; we say you have been productive. One's level of productivity will always determine how much money he or she can make. The more you produce the right results, the more likely it is for money to flow to you.

To be productive is to have the power of producing, of being fertile, fruitful. To be productive is to have the power to bring something into being, causing something to exist, to yield the right results. It is very obvious that man is in need of solutions, so any individual, family, organization and country that can yield the right results, in other words, produce to solve problems, is most likely to see money flowing to their direction.

The above areas are the six major areas money flows to in life. Money as we know flows to some areas in life. Money gravitates. There are some things we need to do and these things will attract money to us. Money does not flow to some areas in life. Money does not flow to where there is idleness, laziness, slothfulness, leisure, and indolence. Money does not flow to people who are unemployed, so please get something to do for yourself. You can employ yourself; you can find something to do for yourself. I challenge you; you can do something for yourself.

Any amount of money you may need can flow to you, what you need to do is to have a product to sell, a skill to provide, a value to add, a knowledge to share, a service to give, an energy to provide and an answer to give to a problem. The next thing to do is to package it in such a way that, more people will be willing to part away an amount of money which is more than the cost of production. Money does not come for the sake of wanting it.

'Allow no sleep to your eyes, no slumber to your eyelids. Free yourself, like a gazelle from the hand of the hunter, like a bird from the snare of the fowler. Go to the ant, you sluggard; consider its ways and be wise. It has no commander, no overseer or ruler, yet it stores its provisions in summer and gathers its food at harvest. How long will you lie there, you sluggard? When will you get up from your sleep? A little sleep, a little slumber, a little folding of the hands to rest and poverty will come on you like a bandit (robber) and scarcity like an armed man'. Proverbs 6:4-11.

As our heading reads, we have six major areas money flows to in life. They could be more areas but we are talking about the MAJOR AREAS.

FACT #9:

Money Is for All of Us (Everyone Can Make It)

Money comes in the form of coins and notes called currency. If you pick any currency, you will realize that no individual's name is written on the money.

This means that money does not belong to a single individual. It belongs to all of us. It can therefore come to you or leave you. You can have it or lose it.

A lot of people have lived their lives believing that money belongs to a group of people and not them. This belief has done great harm to them.

I want to encourage you to know that anyone at all can make enough money. It all depends on you. It is a fact.

Every single note or coin of money in this world is for anyone living in this world. That is why one can come from a different country to your country and start making money in your country.

Anyone at all can have it, provided it is a legal tender. All that the person should do is position themselves well and do the right things that will make money flow to them.

The fact is that anyone at all can make or lose it; it depends on what you do.

FACT #10 :

There Is Nothing Like, 'There Is No Money in The System'

The fact that you do not have enough money does not mean there is no money in the system. The truth is that there has always been enough money in every system, such that if it were shared equally, each one of us could get enough to live on.

Even in the most deprived and poor countries, there are rich men and women. Where did they get their money from? In the same economies and countries where we cry that there is no money, people travel from other places to come and make more of it, taking it back to where they came from.

They got it in the system you are saying has no money. If you want to know about this fact, take a walk through town and visit a shopping mall to see the amount of money that exchanges hands within a minute. You will come to appreciate that there is enough money in every system.

There are also people who have never travelled anywhere but have stayed in the same country and economies where people cry that there is no money, and have become financially independent. The good news is that you can also make it because this money belongs to no one.

Carry this mentality with you always and please stop thinking that there is no money in the system. It will hinder you a lot. What you think makes you. It is a fact.

Chapter Three:

MAKING MONEY

- Facts #11-15: Ordered Environment, Creating Money, Giving Birth, Growth, Equality

FACT #11:

Money Does Not Stay And Grow In A Disordered Environment

As a matter of principle, nothing thrives in a disordered environment, and this applies to money as well. No one can break through financial barriers and make enough money if they do not put their finances in order. Most of us are guilty of impulse buying and excessive spending. The best way to manage your financial life is to plan and budget all your expenses.

Make sure to document all income and expenses, budget your expenses, and try not to exceed your budget. I also recommend window shopping extensively before making a purchase. This can help you buy at a competitive price, leading to savings and financial gains. By following these simple principles, you can take control of your finances and make progress towards your financial goals.

FACT #12:

We Do Not Get Money In Life, Instead We Make Money

I often hear people say 'If I get money, I will do this and that. I have also said it before but the question is, where are you going to get the money, you have not made? Who is going to give you his or her money you have not made? In this part of the world called Africa, we can have people who would give you money as a gift, just some small amount of money you can live on for a day or two but if you want enough sustainable money, there is no way you can get it unless you first make it.

I will advise you to change that wrong way of thinking if you want to walk in sustainable wealth.

FACT #13:

Money Gives Birth To Money

The law of reproduction also applies to money. Your money, no matter how little, can give birth to more money if allowed. By principle, every fruit contains a seed that can reproduce itself. Similarly, every amount of money contains a seed of money.

Wages, salaries, and even gifts of money can be seen as fruits that contain seeds. The fruit is for consumption, while the seed is for planting. Note that this has nothing to do with the size of the seed. Seeds are naturally small. If you want your money to reproduce, it can, but it depends on you.

FACT #14:

Money Grows But Over Time

Just like every seed has the potency to grow, so does money. Your money can be made to grow, but that will be over a period of time. To grow your money, you do not need a big amount to start with; what you need is time and patience.

Remember, seeds are small by nature. No matter how small your money may seem, see it as a seed and invest it, as it has the potential to grow. When we sow a seed, we do not reap a seed; instead, we reap fruits. Also, note that the season we sow a seed is not the same season we reap the fruit. Your money can grow if you allow it.

FACT #15:

Money Is Money Whether Big Or Small

We often think that everything big started big, but that's not the case. Most things we see as big today started small. To me, there is no such thing as small money or big money. It all depends on perception and mindset. What one person considers big, another might not.

The important thing is that every amount of money, whether big or small, is a legal tender that can be used to exchange for goods and services, and therefore has value. Remember, little drops of CONSTANT water can make a mighty ocean. Do not look down on small amounts of money; they have value and can add up to a great value.

Chapter Four

MONEY MANAGEMENT

- Facts #16-20: Means to an End, Creating Assets, Liabilities, Circulation, Spending

FACT #16:

Money Is Only A Means To An End And Not An End In Itself

Money is powerful. The Bible says wisdom is a defence, and so is money. It contains a certain amount and degree of power due to its legal tender status. Therefore, money can empower you to achieve your goals and reach your destination in life. It can help you get fulfilled, make things work out for you quicker, and enable you to do more of what you are capable of.

However, money left alone is not an end in itself. It cannot do anything on its own; its value lies in how one understands and uses it. Money in the hands of a fool, who has no desire to gain wisdom, is of little use. Ultimately, money is a means to an end, not the end itself. It is a tool that can amplify your abilities and help you achieve your goals, but it is not the goal itself.

FACT #17:

Money Is Made by Creating Assets

An asset is anything that brings money to you rather than taking it away from you. The more assets one is able to create, the more money one is likely to make. Again, let me say that it does not matter how small the asset may be, it can create money.

Your skill, time, knowledge, education, qualification, talents, inspiration, and ideas, energy, strategy, connections, and the people you know, the relationships and friendships you have taken time to build, are all assets that can be used to create money.

Lands, gold, cars, buildings, working tools, office equipment, room furniture, household appliances, and anything that can be sold to make money are all assets. The more of such assets you deliberately make, the more money you are likely to make.

The rich use their money to buy things that can bring back the money they used in buying those things. The issue is that, the moment you take out of your pocket to buy something, that money is not yours again. You have used the money to exchange something.

Therefore, in order not to lose the money but rather gain it, whatever you bought or used the money on should directly or indirectly be able to bring the money back to you at any time you want the money. Otherwise, you have lost the money forever.

And we do not become rich by losing money. We become rich by gaining money. To be rich, your money must buy assets. They also allow money to work for them, and that is powerful.

When you allow money to work for you, you get rich faster and also forever, as far as you will allow the money to work. Whenever money is working for you, holidays cannot stop it, weekends cannot stop it, age cannot stop it, and the weather cannot stop it.

That is what makes the rich get richer. Allow your money to work for you.

FACT #18:

Money Is Lost By Creating Liabilities

A liability is anything or person that takes money away from you and does not bring the money back, whether directly or indirectly. Anyone who wants to make enough money should do well to cut down on expenses and also stop creating more liabilities.

There are some unavoidable expenses that we all have to make, such as house and hospital bills, food, transportation, toiletries, soap, cosmetics, etc. However, some expenses can be avoided, like lipsticks, make-ups, perming of hair, wearing, and painting of nails, etc.

The more liabilities you have, the more money you are likely to lose. No two ways about that, it is a fact. The poor use their money to buy things that cannot bring back their money, losing it forever, and that is how we become poor.

Note this: anytime you take money to buy something that cannot bring you back that money, it is a liability, and liabilities make people poor. They work for money instead of allowing money to work for them and become servants to money.

They spend their energy to look for money, and when their energy goes down, their earnings also go down. Weekends, holidays, disasters, and weather changes can all affect their income. If you work for money, your earnings are determined by circumstances, and you have many factors that can hinder your earnings.

"No one can gain or save enough money without enough assets, and no one can lose enough money without enough liabilities. The more assets you have, the more money you gain, and the more liabilities, the more money you lose. The rich acquire assets, while the poor acquire liabilities. The rich allow money to work for them, while the poor work for money."

FACT #19:

Money Does Not Stay At One Place, It Circulates

Because money does not belong to one person, it does not stay at one place for long. This is a fact about money. All foreign currencies were carried around the world by people to transact business, and this points to the fact that money does not stay at one place.

As you read this book, if you bought it, you took money from your pocket to buy it. Where did that money come from, and where is it going? You will notice that money comes to us and then leaves to another person. The rate of circulation is very fast, and one needs wisdom to hold on and keep money for a longer period.

But the issue is, the money you call your own came from someone to you. It was first owned by someone before it became your own, and vice versa. So, it is likely the money will go back to the person it came from, but do not forget that someone else also gave it out to the person who claims ownership of it. Whose money is this particular money then? The one you used in buying this book.

So, do not be much worried that your money is gone to someone; it may come back to you because money circulates. Rather, be worried about what you used the money for.

FACT #20:

Spent Cannot Be a Spending Money Again

Please note that the same amount of money cannot be spent twice. The same money cannot be spent on two things at the same time. It can only be spent once. If you use it to buy something, you cannot use it to buy another thing again.

We often forget this fact, even though we may be aware of it. We are all faced with many needs and a limited amount of money to meet these needs. It is crucial to set our priorities right before we buy, especially if we have a limited amount of money.

It is a fact: money spent on one thing precludes that same money from being spent on something else. Any money spent today or any day can never be available to spend again on any other thing.

I am very particular about this because I have counselled many people on this issue. They get money and soon spend it on things that do not really matter to them. Meanwhile, they have pressing needs that those monies could buy.

Chapter Five:

FINANCIAL MINDSET

- Facts #21-25: Financial Richness, Risk, Medium of Exchange, Keeping Money, Losing Money

FACT #21:

One Needs to Be Financially Rich In The Mind Long Before It Can Manifest Physically

The mind is the mental means to man; all thinking processes take place in the mind. The way one thinks will determine the way one's life will be. Every one of us is just a mind with a body.

Everything we have ever done, all that we are doing now, and can ever do in the future will first have to take place in the mind. In the same way, to be rich financially, one needs to think and act rich first, long before experiencing the riches.

No one can think and act poor and become rich. It does not happen like that. The fact is that we do not have poor people on this earth; rather, we have poor thinkers. That is what makes people poor. As a man thinketh, so is he.

I do not believe there is really a poor person on this earth, looking at the things a human being is made up with. The mind, the brain, the basic qualities, and abilities in mankind alone are full of riches.

I always say that if you can get it in your mind first, it can reflect on your cheque book; if only you get it in your mind first, it is possible to see it reflect in your bank account. No one can be richer than what they think constantly in their mind.

FACT #22:

No Worthwhile Financial Activity Is Totally Devoid of Risk

There is a saying: "No venture, No gain." There is always going to be something for something. No one can receive any financial reward without risk.

The unknown can happen, the unexpected can happen to your investment. However, please do not only fix your mind on the negative; the unknown can also be a big hit than you may expect.

For every financial gain, there is a corresponding degree of risk. The higher the risk, the higher the gain or profit. Becoming financially independent is not just an event, but a process.

One would have to go through a whole lot with calculated risk to become rich. In fact, it is very risky not to risk in anything that has to do with money.

The good news is that all risk can be managed. In doing that, there are two major questions you will need to ask yourself. For more details, get my booklet: "50 Facts About Your Business."

FACT #23:

Money Is Just A Medium Of Exchange

Money is just a medium of exchange, acting as an intermediary between you and the things you want to buy or acquire. In this role, money facilitates the exchange of goods and services. As a result, it plays a crucial part in enabling transactions.

The value of money lies in its ability to unlock access to goods and services. The amount and quality of these goods and services depend on the amount of money you have and are willing to spend. If you do not have enough money, you may not be able to receive what you want. Generally, the more money you have, the better the exchange, and the more you are willing to spend, the better the services you can get. Remember, almost nothing is free, so be prepared to pay for what you want.

FACT #24:

Keeping Money Is More Difficult Than Making It

Even though one may think that making money is difficult, I want to say that keeping money after having made it is far more difficult than the process one has to go through to make it.

It takes a great deal of discipline to resist the temptation of spending on one's appetite. Many seem not to be content with what they have and are always thirsty for more, which requires more spending.

My interaction with people along my line of duty suggests that if men and women will make the effort to kill their appetite for buying and spending, many would in no time break the financial barrier of life.

I have also realized that we have allowed many dependents, peer pressure, social pressure, family pressure, and certain avoidable lifestyles to put high demands on the money we make. Many want to live their lives to please people, so they are not free to take independent decisions. Therefore, keeping money becomes very difficult for them than making it.

Someone will come to me and say, "Rabbi, I make a lot of money but am unable to save," and you will later find out that they are undisciplined in how they spend.

Let me make this clear to you: "To me, true financial security does not lie in the mere possession of money but in the ability to make money anytime it is needed and also having the discipline to make the money stay with you for a long time."

FACT #25:

Losing Money is Much Easier Than Making It

In as much as it will take a great deal of thinking to make money, you would not need to think to lose it. One does not need the same hours he used in making money to lose that money. You can lose money by just being careless, but no one can make money by being careless. You can lose money by being irresponsible, but no one can make money by being irresponsible.

In fact, you do not need to be careful to lose money, but you will need to be very careful to make a little money. Comparatively and competitively, it is more difficult to make money than to lose the same amount of money. A Japanese proverb says that, "To make money is like digging a hole with your nails, and losing money is like pouring water on the sand."

Chapter Six:

BREAKING FINANCIAL BARRIERS

- Facts #26-30: Income, Expenditure, Cause and Effect, Choice, Existing Money

FACT #26:

To Break the Financial Barrier, One's Income Must Exceed His Expenditure

No one can break the financial barrier by spending more than what he is making. It is certain that we would have to pay for almost everything we need, and the same thing applies to others. Therefore, in order for you to break away from poverty, people must pay you more money than you are paying to others.

To break the financial barriers has nothing to do with how much money one is able to make, but how much money one is able to keep. We do not become rich by spending anyhow; rather, we become rich by saving and investing.

The typical Ghanaian and African have a way of demonstrating how rich they are. They spend and spread money to show how much money they have, but in so doing, they become poorer. If you entered a shop with Ghc 100.00 (hundred Ghana Cedis) and by the time you came out of the shop, you had shown to people that you have money by spending just Ghc 10.00 (Ten Ghana Cedis) out of the hundred, you are no more hundred Cedis rich.

You are rather poorer than you entered, even though you have shown to all around you that you have money. Yes, you had, but after spending, you do not.

FACT #27:

All Issues Of Money Is Just Cause And Effect

I always say that there is only one difference between the rich and the poor: knowledge. The reason is that if you see a rich man and a poor man, they both have two eyes, two ears, two hands, two legs, and almost all their physical features are the same.

So, what is it that makes one richer than the other? It is simply what they both know and can do that makes the difference. The rich know something the poor do not know, and therefore, do some things the poor cannot do.

It is cause and effect that makes people rich or poor. The amount of money one is able to make or lose is just the effect of a cause of action. That is why one can be in a deep debt and, by a cause of action, the effect will bring him out of debt.

In the same way, one can be given enough money, but by certain cause of action, the person can run into debt. That is why I totally agree with what the Bible says about getting wisdom on how to make and keep money.

FACT #28:

Poverty Is A Choice And Riches Is A Choice

I always say that people are poor because they have not yet decided to be rich. The day they make that decision, things will begin to change around them.

In the same way, people are rich because they have not yet decided to be poor. The reason is that one needs to make money and be able to hold on to it to be rich financially.

The good news is that the money they will need in order to become rich does not belong to a particular individual; it belongs to all of us. So, what we need is the decision to make it, and that is a choice.

The first corollary law of riches says that, "people become wealthy because they decide to be wealthy". They live to believe that they have the ability to become rich, and so they act accordingly.

FACT #29:

All The Amount Of Money You Need Already Exist

We live in the richest time of all human history. We are surrounded by more wealth and affluence than ever before.

Any amount of money you will need for you to be able to live comfortably on this earth already exists. Your duty is to be able to make your fair share.

This is how I put it: "every one's money is in someone's pocket". Your duty is to identify the person and then take your money out of the person's pocket.

FACT #30:

All Monies Are Eventually Made By Selling Something

Apart from unearned money like gifts, lotteries, inheritance, gambling, etc., selling something directly or indirectly and making a profit is likely to be the major way to making money.

For every business to grow well, it all depends on how much sales the business can make.

Chapter Seven:

SAMRT FINANCIAL DECISIONS

- Facts #31-35: Selling Something, Saving, Long-Term Gains, Financial Intelligence, Expense Reduction

FACT #31:

It Takes More Than Money To Make Money

Even though it takes money to make money, in most cases one will require more than money to make money. That is why one can be totally down financially and within some few months can re-emerge a financial success.

The reason is that it takes more than having money to make money. What you need is a good idea, a good plan of action to your ideas, and finally actions to get things done.

If you can get it in your mind, it can reflect on your cheque book; if you can see it, it can change your bank balance. You will need to be financially rich in your mind long enough before you can actualize it.

What you need most is an idea.

FACT #32:

A Pesewa Saved Is Greater Than A Pesewa Earned

A pesewa is the same as a penny in Ghana. Now what I am saying is that a pesewa saved is greater and has more value than the same pesewa you earned.

The reason is that whenever you save money, that money attracts interest on it and that gives it more value. At the same time, money earned attracts taxes on it and that reduces its value.

One of the ways to earn without being taxed is to make money through savings.

FACT #33:

In The Long Term, Money Is Gained By Buying Durable Things

A lot of people like to buy cheap things, but most of the time, these cheap things are not durable. They are only cheap today but very expensive tomorrow. The reason is that cheap things do not last long because they are not durable. So, you end up buying again several times. On the other hand, durable things are only expensive today, tomorrow they are cheap in the sense that you can use them for a very long time before they get spoiled.

You will realize that the one who buys cheap things might have bought several times, and the total cost would exceed that of the durable one. So, in the long run, cheap things turn out to be expensive and thus make us lose money. While durable things turn out to be cheap and less expensive in the long run, and this makes us gain money.

FACT #34:

To Break The Financial Barrier, One Needs To Be Financially Intelligent

Learn and know much about money; no one can do what he or she does not know. You can only do what you know. In most cases, it is not how much money one gets that matters but how much knowledge one has in managing the money at hand.

The Bible says in the book Proverbs 17:16, *"Of what use is money in the hand of a fool, since he has no desire to get wisdom?"* (NET) Over here, the word fool is not the one who is foolish in itself but the one who lacks wisdom in how to manage money.

Knowledge, they say, is power; application of knowledge is important in all that we do. The Bible says it is the principal thing. No one can do above what he or she knows. If you can do much financially, then you have to know much financially.

FACT #35:

Cut Down On Your Expenses Where Necessary

We can all see that there are a lot of expenses we do that are not very necessary and do not add anything to our lives. We sometimes buysome things and later realize we do not need them.

Some of these items lie down for a long time without being used. There are also some things we buy but can do without them; we do not really need them. We can cut down on all those purchases and save or invest the money.

The habit where we have to always spend everything we make must stop. If it will be possible, let us cut down on what we spend our monies on. This will go a long way to help us gain money than lose it.

Chapter Eight:

INVESTMENT STRATEGIES

Facts #36-43: Limiting Losses, Delayed Gratification, Inflation Hedge, Risky Commodities, Liquid Assets, Passive Investment

FACT #36

Try To Limit Your Losses

Because we are human beings, we cannot be perfect in all that we do. Some of the times, we may do some mistakes and this can result into losses. Some of the losses can be very expensive and can become liabilities to us.

This will make us lose money instead of gaining money. Whenever you lose, you have lost; it is not a gain. You can bear with me that, no matter how little those losses may be, many of such little losses when put together, can be huge.

That is why it is very important for us to do our best to limit or reduce some of these losses. Remember this saying; 'penny wise, Pound foolish'.

FACT #37:

Delay Your Gratification

Most of the time when people work and start making profit, when they start prospering and the business is doing well, they immediately reward themselves and start having pleasure.

In so doing, they buy expensive cars, dresses, visit expensive restaurants, and they begin to spend, and that is how they turn to lose money. It is this kind of lifestyle that I am saying to delay.

It is good to enjoy the fruit of your labour, but you can choose to delay it so you can create more assets. Remember, our aim here is to gain money, not to lose money.

FACT #38:

Stop Buying "Assets" That Do Not Perform

Most of the time, we use the little money on us to buy some assets that are not able to perform. They come to sit without bringing us any income.

These types of assets are not assets but are rather liabilities. The reason is that those assets have taken money out from you and bring in nothing. They do not function; they are more of a disadvantage than advantage.

Instead, we should cultivate the habit of buying things that help us gain money than lose them. We should prioritize investing in assets that generate income, appreciate in value, or provide a strong potential for long-term growth.

FACT #39:

Invest In Assets That Are Inflation Hedge

There are some investments that can be affected by inflation. When that happens, you are bound to lose some good money.

Some properties like lands, gold, buildings, etc. are inflation hedge. These assets are not affected negatively by inflation, and when you have them, you rather gain money than lose them.

This kind of business is good in countries with very unstable rising inflation. Investing in assets that are resistant to inflation can help protect your wealth and even provide a potential for growth during periods of high inflation.

FACT #40:

Do Not Invest In Risky Commodities

Some investments are risky, and one should be very careful in putting money into such investments, especially with our little working capital or the only money on you.

For instance, I will not advise you to use all the money on you to buy a commodity like a car for commercial purposes. It has a high-risk tendency; it is not advisable at all.

In such instances, if you lose, it will be a great loss. But please do not lose money, gain it. It is essential to assess the risk involved and consider diversifying your investments to minimize potential losses. Always prioritize cautious and informed investment decisions to protect your financial resources.

FACT #41:

Invest Into High Consumables Items

Some items have a high rate of consumption, and when you invest in such commodities, you are likely to double your capital in a short period.

In most cases, these items differ from place to place. The items that may be consumed much in a particular location may not necessarily have the same rate of consumption elsewhere.

Over here, it is up to you to study the market to know which items will move faster. Conducting market research and analysing consumer demand can help you identify high-consumable items that can yield a good return on investment.

FACT #42:

Invest Into Liquid Assets

Some assets are able to fetch us cash faster than others. Assets like tractors, bulldozers, heavy equipment, etc. are not liquid assets because they are not normally easy to sell to get cash quickly.

On the other hand, a commodity like gold is a liquid asset. It is an item you can easily turn into cash. To avoid having your money locked up in an asset, it is advisable to invest in liquid assets.

Another advantage of liquid assets is that, anytime you are deeply in need of money for an urgent purpose, you can easily turn your liquid asset into cash. This provides a sense of security and flexibility in managing your finances.

FACT #43:

Try To Do Passive Investment

A passive investment is a type of investment that does not require much of your time or personal involvement. In other words, you can invest and still have time for other activities or businesses.

Examples of passive investments include farming, treasury bills, and buying shares. These investments can generate income without requiring constant monitoring or direct involvement.

Passive investment is advantageous for those who are already occupied with other commitments but still want to grow their wealth. It allows you to create additional assets that can generate income, providing financial stability and security.

Chapter Nine:

WEALTH BUILDING

- Facts #44-48: Loan Repayment, Investment Completion, Respect for Money, Difficulty of Making Money

FACT #44:

Accelerate All Loans Repayment

You will agree with me that most loans attract interest. Therefore, if you delay repaying the loan, the interest you pay will increase, resulting in financial losses.

When you delay loan repayment, you ultimately lose money, especially if the loan comes with interest. Initially, you lose money by paying for the loan and its interest. If you delay, you will end up paying more than you should.

To minimize losses, it is essential to accelerate loan repayment, paying off the principal amount and interest as quickly as possible. This will help you save money and avoid further financial burdens.

FACT #45:

Do not Leave Your Investments Half Way

Many people invest money in a business but leave it unfinished, which defeats the purpose of investing in the first place. If you are investing, it is likely for profit. However, how can you make a profit if you leave the investment halfway?

When you abandon an investment, you lock up capital and lose money. For instance, someone might start a small store but leave it unfinished due to lack of funds. Instead of completing the initial project when they have more money, they might start a new one from scratch. This leads to financial losses instead of gains.

It is essential to see your investments through to completion to reap the rewards and avoid wasting resources.

FACT #46:

Treat Every Money You Make In The Following Three Ways

As A Worker, An Asset and A Customer.

1. **Money As a Worker:** We employ workers to work for us and pay them at the end of the month. In the same way, let your money work for you and after the money has done the work for you, pay your money a salary.

So, for instance, if you have in your hands one million cedis, let that one million cedis work for you and when the profit comes, take out of the profit and pay the one million cedis a salary. Continue this cycle and in no time, you will see your money growing.

Workers are supposed to work but after they have worked for us, we are also supposed to pay them. That is how we must all treat every money that comes into our hand.

50 FACTS ABOUT MONEY

2. Money As an Asset: Assets by our definition are to bring us money. An asset brings us money and that is how every money we get is supposed to do for us. But we have to cause that to happen.

So, the money you get must be treated in such a way that, it will put money into your pocket. That money you get must be to your advantage. If we do that, we gain money instead of losing money.

3. Money As a Customer: As a customer, because our customers keep us in business. Customers pay for our goods and services; they also supply and bring us more business.

It is because of our customers that our businesses keep on running. These customers are very important to us. We treat them with respect and care.

That is how we are to treat and see the monies that come into our hand. You must treat the money in such a way that, no matter how small that amount may be, it will keep you in business.

That money must get you more money, more goods, more supply and more services. These are the characteristics of a customer.

FACT #47:

Respect Every Pesewa Or Cent

There is a saying that goes this way: little drops of water make a mighty ocean. Penny wise, pound foolish. Every single pesewa matters in our financial issues.

Do not cultivate the habit of losing little monies because little things eventually turn out to become big. So, in effect, it is no longer little monies you lose but big ones.

Every money is money, whether little or big. Respect it, and you will be shocked at what will come out of it. By valuing every small amount, you can make a significant impact on your financial situation and achieve your goals.

FACT #48:

It Is More Difficult To Make Money Than To Lose The Same Amount Of Money

If you consider carefully, you will realize that it is more difficult for one to make money than to lose it. The difficulty one would have to go through, the degree of thinking one would have to do before he or she is able to make a little amount of money, it will be very important we behave in such a way that we do not lose the money so easily.

Let me ask you these questions; how does money come in and how does it go out, secondly, the rate at which money comes in, is it at the same rate that the money goes out and thirdly, the amount of money that comes in, is it the same amount of money that usually goes out?

In the first place, you will realize that the way money comes in is not the way the same money goes out.

Secondly, you will also notice that the rate at which money comes in is not the same rate at which that money goes out and lastly, the amount of money that comes in is most of the time lesser than the one that goes out.

That is why we always lack or lose money. It is therefore a fact that money is more difficult to make than to lose it. The rate at which we gain money is far slower than the rate at which we lose the same money.

What we do to lose money is little compared to the things we do to gain the same amount of money. The avenues we have that money flows through to us are lesser than the avenues that take the same amount of money away from us and it is sad to say that we are responsible for all these.

We are the ones who create both channels, the ones that bring in the money and the ones that take out the money.

Chapter Ten

FINANCIAL DISCIPLINE

Facts #49-50: Buying What You Need, Taking Action

FACT #49:

Buy Only What You Need

Most of the time, we buy some things and they stay there for a longer period without use. You see that we do not really need those things but we bought them, meanwhile, we complain that we need money for other things.

Some of us complain we need capital but we use the very money that could have served as a capital to buy things that lie down for years without using those things. We lose money by doing that.

So instead of those items serving as assets, they now become liabilities. They have taken money from you and are not bringing it back.

Let us cultivate that habit of buying only what we need at a time. By doing so, we can avoid unnecessary expenses and make the most of our money.

FACT #50:

If You Cannot Do Any Of The Above, Do What Is Below

Try to work for all that you will need. Do not spend what you have not worked for. We cannot lose financially; rather, we have to win or gain money. And where we cannot gain, we must not lose as well.

That is why it is important for us to try to live within our means. In conclusion, let me encourage you by saying that each and every one can attain true financial freedom; everyone can be rich and wealthy.

It all starts with a deep and sincere desire to become financially free. No one can be rich carrying a weak desire; your desire to become rich must be very strong and unshakable.

You must be willing to make all the sacrifices that need to be done. The next thing or quality you need to become financially free is to decide to do what must be done to be rich and wealthy.

You need to make a strong, firm, and clear decision that you are going to do all that it takes to become rich. There must not be shadows of doubt in your decision making.

It must be so strong that nothing can make you change your mind. Thirdly, you must be very determined to succeed.

In other words, you are going to work at it till you succeed at the decision you have taken. To be determined means you are not going to give up on your dream of becoming rich in spite of all the difficulties, challenges, problems, and the obstacles that may come your way.

You can only make it if you persevere no matter what. The fourth thing you have to do is to practice self-discipline; doing the very things that must be done even when you do not feel like doing them.

It means you have to work hard to develop the habits necessary for achieving your dream of becoming financially free.

'Wisdom is supreme; therefore, get wisdom. Though it cost all you have, get understanding.' Proverbs 4:7

Stay tuned for Volume 2 of '50 Facts About Money', coming soon!

Keep on learning, because you can only do what you know and it is only what you know that will make you.

There is a saying that goes like this; if you take out of your pocket into your head, your head will pay your pocket back after many days.

If you learn, you have invested and you will never regret you did.

Let us also consider what the Bible says about money and wisdom. Proverbs 17:16 *'Of what use is money in the hands of a fool, since he has no desire to get wisdom?'* (NET).

I will recommend that we do our best to acquire wisdom in managing every little pesewa that we make in the same way as we do our best to make the pesewa.

It is true that anyone who cannot manage little money cannot manage much. We need wisdom before money.

I know one will say give me money and I will get the wisdom to manage it.

You see, money will only come in to empower you to do what you are already made of. Money does not give us wisdom; rather, it gives the ability to do what we know already.

So, if you are not wise when it comes to issues of money as the Bible is saying, what money will do to you is to help or empower you to act foolishly.

Of what use is money in the hands of a fool.

CONTACT US:

✍ **Write to us at:**
P. O. Box NK 225,
North Kaneshie,
Accra, Ghana

✉ **Email us at:**
schoolofdestiny@yahoo.com
odameansa@gmail.com
Facebook: @ Samuel Odame-Ansa
TikTok @ Rabbi Odame-Ansa

☎ **Call us at:**
+233-242560562
+233-275858710

📖 Other Books by Rabbi Samuel Odame-Ansa:
- The 50 Facts about Life
- The Fundamental Principles of Life and Destiny

www.ingramcontent.com/pod-product-compliance
Lightning Source LLC
Chambersburg PA
CBHW070200230526
45471CB00002B/746